SALVAGE

CYNTHIA DEWI OKA

SALVAGE

POEMS

TRIQUARTERLY BOOKS/NORTHWESTERN UNIVERSITY PRESS

EVANSTON, ILLINOIS

TriQuarterly Books
Northwestern University Press
www.nupress.northwestern.edu

Copyright © 2018 by Cynthia Dewi Oka. Published 2018
by TriQuarterly Books/Northwestern University Press.
All rights reserved.

Printed in the United States of America

10   9   8   7   6   5   4   3   2   1

Library of Congress Cataloging-in-Publication Data
Names: Oka, Cynthia Dewi, author.
Title: Salvage : poems / Cynthia Dewi Oka.
Description: Evanston, Illinois : TriQuarterly Books/Northwestern University Press, 2017.
Identifiers: LCCN 2017022790 | ISBN 9780810136298 (pbk. : alk. paper) |
   ISBN 9780810136304 (e-book)
Classification: LCC PS3615.K33 S25 2017 | DDC 811.6—dc23
LC record available at https://lccn.loc.gov/2017022790

For Paulus

I stroke the beam of my lamp
slowly along the flank
of something more permanent
than fish or weed

the thing I came for:
the wreck and not the story of the wreck
the thing itself and not the myth
    —Adrienne Rich, "Diving into the Wreck"

You will be lost.
You'll create a room with no walls.
    —Abd El-Monem Ramadan,
     "Preparation for Our Desires"

Contents

HOWL IN OUR HANDS

SALVAGE

MERAPI

In the clay yard of childhood, my aunt
bloodied and soot-kissed, sheds her clothes
upon the mossy lip of a well. An offering

rinsed in dawn's coral light, the steam
rising off a fresh kill. Her hands clutch
the tar-bound rope, each vein a thick blue

knot hoisting bucket after bucket of dutiful
libation. With each drop night's omen
returned to the lightless eye of water.

Though afraid I do not resist her
or the cry of the muezzin like a cold blade
against my skin. I want to touch them all—

burnt patches, pale worms pleating
breasts and belly, the shadowy rooms
of slaughter. How each gesture glistens

in memory like a scar. Years later
they will find her, dead behind a door no one
thinks to open until the stench of rotting

flesh seeps through the brick walls.
I will not weep or fly home, burying only
that morning when small and naked

I stand with her marveling in the cool
breeze, like goddesses, exposed
beyond the avarice of beauty

as the volcano hemorrhages
its viscera above us. Tracing wrack
lines where the sun has dried

moments before we brush them away—
cicada wing on an elbow, salam leaf
on a thigh—evidence of unrequited

thirsts. Accidental drownings. The body's
risk: believing I am stronger than
the silence which swarms like beetles

around my heart. Clamber. Break
apart. Spill—
I do not hear the eruption when it happens.

Boiling lakes of mud and falling
timber. Bones catching fire.
The refugees we suddenly become.

Even now I tell myself I've escaped
the magma's gambit; the lucky one
looking for God in the ashes.

WHAT IS BELIEVED OF PARADISE

Because there is no refuge
there is refuge.
> —Adam Zagajewski, "In the Past"

THOUGH WE'VE NO CHANCE OF ESCAPE, ENCORE

And does it matter that we do not know
what to call ourselves? That finally,
a house is not a poem, a border is not

      a stitch in the earth? That beneath, upon
      our skin molders centuries of the furious

machine—dislocation, amnesia, ransack?
The rain guitars us to leaves of grass
along Camden's waterfront—you, me,

      ghosts of our slanderous past taking
      root in potholed sidewalks, the striated

glare of passing cars. How heavy the nights
anchored to our ribs from which we
wrestled our luminous darknesses; how

      desperately we grope for insinuations
      of welcome—rock wire graffiti—signs

that injury is what happened to make
of absence a place. Stumbling toward
the clock at the river's edge, blinded

      in sheets of water, we move like twilight—
      block after block howling the murk

of all that has lived and drowned
in the impossible music of our blood.
The knife's narrative will always

    summon us into the loneliness of history,
    but today the sky drums, even the brick

walls of the penitentiary are anointed.

ISHTAR IN SUBURBIA

According to the Bureau of Investigative Journalism, as of
May 2016, the United States has carried out 423 drone strikes
in Pakistan, with a reported death toll ranging from 2,498 to
3,999 people. Hundreds more strikes have been carried out in
Afghanistan, Yemen, and Somalia.

Then face.
Then sheets of dust.
Then black splinters of sun.
Whir. Enormous mosquitoes.
The bowels release.
Then empire

~

There is a way to cleanse the sex out of war.
I mean libido, lick. The funk
& nasty. The sweat-paste, moaning
hair

~

Then coffee.
Then towelette.
Then fingernails chewed to the quick.
Razors of asphalt.
The bony woman whose job it is to usher traffic at the crosswalk.
Splay of metal. Then bloat.
The morning like chalk.

ENTER: *The only Mexicans in the neighborhood leap out of the back of the garbage collec-*
tion truck, bright orange latex gloves flapping in their jeans' pockets

~

You ride the train downtown.
Past fields of crow-picked rubble. Charred row houses
Their windows missing like teeth.
Then the stadium. The gleaming university.
You cross high above water.
It should unsettle, exhilarate
This intuition of thunder
Tunnels like the black mane of an Arabian horse.
But this is common. Skin on skin.
Eyes fractions of an inch apart. At each stop
More flood in. The car fills to bursting.
The pressure thickens. Intimate & putrid
Scents. Then flesh humming
Against flesh

~

You can imagine the component parts.
Mortar, shingle, tire, goat. The areas cleared for kickball.
Words like *convoy* and *wind resistance*.
Then inferno
Wildflower
Then hands like wick

~

Rewind. The *Times* wrapped around meat and bread.

ENTER: John. Your neighbor, a Freemason in his sixties. He brought over a bottle of wine when you first moved here. You discuss the prolonged chill. His son's recovery. His girl-friend's country house in _____. *He still can't remember your name*

~

Then a study of identity in the spackled mirror.
Then not wanting to know the names of the dead.
Then guilt, then departure.
Then a pact with the mulberries crushed into pavement.
Then driving through the cemetery for its view of the stars.
Then remembering to dig.

FOR KHALIL, FIRST RESPONDER, WHOSE NAME MEANS "FRIEND"

I pray peace is with you Angel
who haunts the elm-lined boulevards   America's
cologne-bright   pools of unseeing
blue   in whose name Hellfire
becomes God's

infrared spring   the Heart's
globe of hornets   ground that spurts
like a vein   your love Khalil like History's darkling
fruit   *so burnt you can't tell*
cattle from human   how did you carry

what you found & crawl thru
the gorged Hippocampus   in whose name
Boy becomes hearse   this birthmark that hill
of bone   is it real did the missile do it
such thirst Khalil   among

flies that crust the arm   once
bridge between   cup & cards stowed inside
the sleeve's   Holy   color which saves
none from sundering   hum
that halves the crown   *there*

is pain in his head   like wheat
in Sand   or centers of palms
unfisting for   the blackened ingots
of body   *we will ask nothing*
of you Khalil   but this parting

of the hecatomb when the sierra breaks
like an old Lion's back   Our fear
the cargo of everyday gestures like this
poem I am failing   to wedge
between you & the sky   in time

when I pray   it is leaves
swelling the bellies of goats   the quarry
of divided futures   though we live & vanish
Song is not   stronger than iron
in the pit in the white

strips of what was & who   should have
continued *no matter what*
This ash & not-ash
staining jaw   breath   the every sunlight
that enters   you as Refuge

THE AMERICAN DREAM WRITES TO ORPHEUS

My love,
The tide is poised. Between you and I the end of the world

where an abandoned crane will either spit blue
blazing desert from its graffiti lips or smash
the crow-bedecked tenements in search of a trumpet.

I am somewhere the horizon is slippery, quartered;
a compost of insurrections mirroring the body.
I am somewhere famished for a bare face.

The Hellfire travels 995 miles per hour. Where it lands, soul
is freed like fire through skin, touching dirt for the first time.

A maggot's labor, like yours, is apostolic.

I'd like to tell you I've learned something of patience. Watching for
birds in the flash of windows beneath the eyelids, the wrist
in darkening sand. Are we really that different?

I am somewhere the shards of a wine jar,
the coal on a mother's brow.
I am somewhere deafened by wings.

You believe no shadow is lost, ever only searching
for sound. Each continent begins with a cloud and is forever

caesura. But have you felt kingdoms roll below you,
your back the red sun in that gloaming hour
when all the world's eyes closed, close upon you?

Forgive me. Such a thin and treacherous margin
this drinking, singing river of heads,
this dying, singing river of breath.

LAZARUS RECONSIDERS HIS AWAKENING

What of boulders the Lord does not command to move
aside, the blood-pollen on azure spring and bones
marked to splinter the hooves of cattle? From a drone's
teeth, black spittle of mountains, the fugitive proof.
How our Lord, enthralled by your firework, aloof,
stoops in the mud like a house of overdue loans—
his love syringed, his floorboards smooth. A bowl of moans,
the hushed bell hushing swallows in the body's groove.

What of the animal, ritual and meta-
phor of need, you become—beheld by flame? Filled
at last with flutes, with prophecy, the holy brain
crawls its way up the leaves, feeling out the junta
of titanium-studded night. O rose's hilt,
resurrection, which tomb beyond the flag's refrain?

ELEGY FOR THE HELLFIRE

without sleep without history   † † † †
                   the first thing

     red dot that is flesh   sand's infinite   miracle, cleft

    & skin's brittle leaf   † † † † wave   *without sound without*

memory of sound   stone-wrench mountain-blood

       the bobbing globes   † † † †   of lung   O, torn

O, praise the black steam   body! rinsed to powder   without apparition

                   † † † †
         and the animals let loose   dream-blister   moon–

   glass   scorched reason, flag of the living   nothing heals

    † † † †   this tundra of light   not rose   abstraction

what is believed of paradise.   *locust and palm without*   † † † †

fruit without water   the first sparrow filled

       with breaking   O, ear
                  † † † †

O, salt-pyre   let me taste

my memories like fish   without a place to begin ✝ ✝ ✝ ✝   without

salvation.

The italicized lines above are from Laurie Lamon's poem "Pain Thinks of the First Thing," in *The Fork Without Hunger*.

ORPHEUS IS MUGGED IN THE CITY OF BROTHERLY LOVE

At 8th and Market the lost line
of a jeremiad, caught in a woman's throat, ad infinitum
a dollar for the homeless . . .

a desert stretched over the drum's hollow
inside which a god forgets
he is a god, a shriek

through damp tunnels,
through which doors pass and light and pupils
—so much feels

like church, city bending the nape,
hook in your shoulders, and everywhere, hunger.
The shadow evil casts: if

three stops from now a man puts his hand
on you and wrests
your identity, hard-earned bread

and you throw your weight on him like the spirit,
like the rocking
and hold

until the smell of burning fills
your mouth, the crowd silent, enraptured by
the miracle of need

pressed against need, will you call him brother
as he limps away, coal-smudge
on the oneness of winter, needle, dagger, you

who've never seen his face
yet praise love so easily, the sun, crows nailing
the wind, a whole kingdom's

teeth scraped on coins

GARDEN STATE

Sunset. Bellies empty we glide
into summer, slit by fireflies. Muslin fluorescence.
Cops & cabbies in glades of smoke. The streets
panoptic. The brick of our bones thinking
of rain. Newport conspiracies. Espionage,
entry

> *god of torn membranes, god of imagined lives*
> *eating palm-shadows on dustless patios*
> *god of geranium & African violet*
> *god of the promise of harbor*

A candle for each moth. The shutters of nostalgia.
Rooms to smuggle horizons & grandfather clocks.
Fingers, pearl studded force. Armoire
of regrets. Garden gnomes then dogs
in the turned over earth. Our silhouettes
like blow

> *god of the besieged, god of mug shots*
> *taken by streetlight, god of waste bins*
> *squeezed like men waiting furiously for work*
> *god of phantom-limbed refusals*

The oak explodes. Veins over roofs. Ink spilled
on faded-jeans sky & salmon. Clouds,
memories of the last great fire. White-socked Teresa
of Calcutta. The parish where desire thieves
our hands & spins. A fifties
black and white

god of hypothetical verandas
god of halcyon days are over
god of waxed skin & fishnet kisses all year
Dancing with the Stars, god of merciful

amnesia, in bodies of trespass, hallowed be thy name

AFTER HURRICANE SANDY

We climb toward the rumored grave
of a Native American healer, the earth
a vertigo of blackness and exposed
root beneath our palms, pressing up
through the waves of molten leaves,
toward the bluff where our children,
having for the past hour pretended
not to hear our demands for them
to come down, are now balancing
their sun-licked, baby-fat-all-but-gone
bodies on a thin shelf of rock. "Look,
it's a deer! A deer in a wolf's face!"
Their cries tumble down, snagging
like runaway rags on the branches;
they look like Brutus and Cassius
debating the fate and meaning of
a red stain the size of a man etched
into granite, commanding the speech
of minerals—they've found a myth
worth more than their mothers' fear.
The wind makes a bear of me, gristling
my chest and thighs as I crawl, gravity
inhaling me like an enormous throat,
over the deadness of trees and thorned
bushes, knuckles bursting like berries,
thoughts detritus around a *New York
Post* article I read about a woman who,
weeks ago, her brain sweaty with prayer,
climbed the rope of her body, her black
body, up the steepest mountain in America,
which rose between the door of her car

where her children rocked each other
in the arms of the storm and the door
of the house she knocked and knocked,
until her knuckles burst into mouths,
her body a black tongue, a root burning
against which the family in the living room
drily surveyed their possessions:
fine china, paintings collected over
the years, utensils gleaming in candlelight,
the life-size television—their window
into loss and destruction—which
is silent now, their sleeping Noah.
The door did not open. The animals in
the house survived, while two baby boys
washed away, their screams become
the moulted skin of water as it bucked,
roiled against its own vanishing empire,
claiming for days a solid mass, blitzkrieg
of porches and tire swings, of libraries,
the vowels of a child's eyes looking up
at the body that broke open for him
and keeps breaking, like a faulty dam,
even after water returns to water, lifting
like souls in sunlight, to form the clouds
that now drift above us, waiting their turn
to kiss the mouth of a forgotten grave,
the red of a mother's heart. I hold my son
to me, I breathe him, and try to witness
the miracle of leaves still clinging
to branches, scrawling their petitions
on the November breeze—even as we
stare at our knuckles, the ripe strength
of them, on this precipice we have been
led to in the wake of the flood, asking
the gods, which do we raise them to be:
deer or wolf? The dead give nothing away.

THE MEN WHO TURNED INTO AIR

circled caverns of broad daylight

where no two souls speak   the same inferno
hope glinted on sidewalks like needles   & burst
condoms   you think you know the lyrics

big-knuckled boys   chinning up to challenge
one hundred feet above glimmer

messiah of pavement   *wassup brotha, keep ya head up*

chalk & sheer belief   the sun begins to drown
in the red net of city   balloons drift   humans
& windows opening

                                        we was made

detonated you think you know   sin must be
inevitable   color their skin   *in the image of god*

this middle of room where love was made

& vodka spilled   negligent means by which cleave
slipped in   then through   doubling as good-bye
you were almost there when their mirrors broke

listen   sometimes pretend to be
stronger than the rain clinging you   like hurt

singing *please, please   put your mouth around my song*

NOM DE GUERRE

From July 11 to September 26, 1990, the Kahnien'kehaka community of Kanehsatake defended their sacred pine grove and burial grounds against the colonial forces of the Sûreté du Québec, the Royal Canadian Mounted Police, and the Canadian Armed Forces, which were enforcing the expansion of an exclusive golf club and luxury condos by the city of Oka, Quebec.

Still the pines sing where you bury your dead.
Beneath groves of tire and history's plank,
your souls the sun in this nation of lead.

Grow into shrub, into thorn, what is bled
to pierce horizon's manicured flank
where pines have buried their songs of the dead.

Chase truth to her lair, *avenge us!* they said.
Tumbling, encircled, wildflowers you sank.
The blades churning sky, a fever of lead.

You rise with the night. You rise through the dread,
besiege the colony's murderous rank.
O, pinesongs, you! Refuse to be dead!

Not of you, and yet, I follow your stead.
Fashion of tongue-page, a glistening shank
to strip the nation's soul-armor of lead.

Who made of clouds and gunfire a shed,
of opened veins the bright spring that you drank?
The pines still sing where you bury your dead.
Your love, the sun on this planet of lead.

ANTHEM

In remembrance of the missing and murdered women of the
Downtown Eastside

—FEBRUARY 14 ANNUAL MEMORIAL MARCH, VANCOUVER,
COAST SALISH TERRITORIES

we are called to the wind / our throat
      unleashes / robe feather bannock
our bodies / beneath / the heat
      of the drum

              there is a war on our lives / a war
                  on our lives it looks like / pressed
              suits and Kevlar / double-decker
                    hearts / vintage / everything

is plunder / police-manned / rooftops
      siege / of eagle and her / mercy we
come to bless / asphalt / soul's
      rain-pressed alleys / the blood—

              thirst in husks of tongue / we / who wait
                  all our lives / to be / safe
              in the quilts of our names / our dance
                  lightning / our breath / forbidden

street in death-row / city / no more
      fallen / no more / graves in air sawed
by silence / skin the sun / sing
      the drums that raise / the dead

JESUS IS TESTED IN THE DOWNTOWN EASTSIDE

Nowhere is the devil to be found. Only windows of Superman dust. Brick facades
like the thighs of old men. Cardboard condos swaying on the banks of rush hour traffic.
This is no desert though on bad days the matchstick light fills the body with sand.
No miracle is required. Only, snuff out the night's fire with gloved hands. The visceral
snap of an umbrella (like palm over mouth). Under dry-cleaned coats there are months
of rain. Calendars chalked on the macadam. Bones crumpled like paper. The women
work the darkness like breaking a horse, reciting the names of the missing like medicine.
Now the leaves cease to imitate fever and socks are difficult to come by. Now
the police grow wings over their blue shells. *Tut-tut-tut* they strut—hip, enameled
royalty. I'm not depressed. The coffee is decent at Main and Columbia. The road back
to innocence is needle-thin. And at any hour, there are carts unzipping sidewalks
loaded with the castoffs a life is trying to salvage. See the bright scarves of flesh?
Slender fingers clipping a morning's first cigarette? After a thunderstorm, the sky
is red as nostalgia. I stand beneath it, naked. Naked as the way humans love on
this roach-infested, pedestrian earth. Sometimes I imagine it's my face on the semen—,
bloodstained bills that pass hand to hand like the poor man's Olympic torch.
But it rains too often to keep up the mirage, and so even deities learn. This is pain.
This is power. This is the hand of a child I am holding, who suddenly disappears.

SMALL STUBBORN GODS

Homeland, I am not your mother,
so why do you weep in my lap like this
every time
something hurts you?
  —Dunya Mikhail, "Tablets"

HOW TO WATCH *THE ACT OF KILLING*

Remember this isn't real.

Though the fires laugh redly & the bamboo bleeds.
Black crowns of tualang trees & birds fall
like sleet. Beneath the shamed sun houses
shudder like goats at the stockyard.

Though the women's faces purple,
their thighs licked by flames like corn husks.
Machetes wink & children's mouths gape like eyes.
This is not the mathematic scene of torture
nor the wire's political restraint—

you must believe

what is not really happening. Angels of death
rocking coal-flesh against their breasts, lips
kissing away terror's foam, anointing
brows with cigar smoke.
Now the ones who play the prey—grandchildren & neighbors,

strangers and childhood friends—stare
sphinxlike through the screen. A make-believe memory,
myth shaped like a wail
looking for the body it belongs to.

Is this what you mean when you say *homeland*?
When you say *heal* & touch
please, *these nerve-ends of separation*?

Remember you are not there
whipped by the patriotic winds, imprinted
in sulfur, though you are
a child of the act of burning,
a child lost and smuggled to the seated side of the screen:

You must open your hands & hold

the fate that is yours,
which isn't to decide who lives or dies or where
metaphor ends & pain is demoted
back to unthinkable pain, but to look again & again

at this blood of initiation, the hatred
that brought you here & stoops now
an old man behind the camera, sleepless, immaculate
in his suit & fedora surveying the great fresco of his life

your libraries of Anonymous,
your sparrow-less, silent world.

In *The Act of Killing*, a documentary about the mass killings of 1965–66 in Indonesia
that targeted suspected communists, trade unionists, intellectuals, landless peasants, and
Chinese Indonesians, filmmakers challenged death squad leaders to reenact their real-life
executions in the style of their favorite American movies.

SELF-PORTRAIT AS ONE DAY ON MY HOME ISLAND OF BALI

—In memory of Chairil Anwar (1922–1949)

(*breath*)
vigil of baskets
woven of yearning under
the tamarind sun

~

(*temple*)
from banana leaves,
tin roofs, sap-white bones, scatters
rain like prayer beads

~

(*hunger*)
women crouch in smoky
irises, their faces peel
darkly, fluorescent

~

(*language*)
wind buffeting sheets
along the clothesline, the bees'
bristled opera

~

(*wound*)
a boy holds out dirt—
cracked palms, my face collects dust
in his cavern eyes

~

(*history*)
marauding tourists
street children, a penny-wish
in the cheeks of dusk

~

(*memory*)
the body doing
what the body must, which is
release, rampart, scar

~

(*nation*)
albatross over
fire-baptized sea, searching
for place to alight

~

(*song*)
tethered by a thread
climb and strain like kites, laughing
mystics of the night

SUPPOSE YOU WERE A KOMODO DRAGON

Yellow-tongued incubus & graveyard
mercenary. Armor of hardened dust. The music-
less plow through earth's gauntlet of flies.

Suppose beneath eyelids of stone, you never
tried to resist your fate. To sabotage all attempts
at flight. All flesh lambent & flaking

to memory. Each sun-burnished link
in bloodlines of need you've chewed with titanic
relish. Suppose God were a big toothy

chamber inside you. Swallowing all day
even as the breeze turns your head with news
of fresh carrion. Venom & bravado are

your deliverance in ambush, but then
you lie, supine in the heat, feeling ghosts move slow
& unyielding through you. Yes,

you've looked over extinction's edge.
Silently cursed your resilience amidst the liquid
bones & star-stricken panic. As much

sacrilege as the migrations you incite,
the rocks you make us pile on our dead. In captivity,
you'll eat whatever you're served.

Suppose none of us got here by choice,
just by the strength of our longing & greed
to recalibrate patterns of separation.

Suppose the land like the body broke
apart, without a way to return. Like you, we might
evolve into the meanest cleanup crew

there ever was. Meet the night's tusk
with the shank of our skin. Have *stranded*
like a pincer in our blood. We'll fight

all our lives to work for nothing
more than a godforsaken hole in the ground,
a totem of regret.

ELEGY FOR RED: A *ZUIHITSU*

1
Paper, spark, mouth. The closest I've been to a star.

2
"The last thing addicts are afraid of is death," writes poet Benjamin Alire Sáenz.

3
The neon stiletto in a triple X store window stabs the cornea. Something akin to agony breathes me through its unblinking frame.

4
As a child, I watched desire morph into sentence; a thin, long wire around my father's heart.

5
What the mind wears in readiness/defiance of its own disappearance. Shroud. Banner. Bandage. The bull of the world raises its horns.

6
At sunrise, before the news, *Allah hu akbar* sailing through windows and rooftops, announcing safe passage through the realm of illusion.

7
Angpau of salt-veined dollar bills, also known as notes from the underground.

8
Cardinal's plume on a bed of a frost, Chinese lanterns bobbing on the River Styx: the immigrant's refrain pulsing toward loss—borderless country, Promised Land.

9
Lipstick smear. Centuries. A dark girl parting a dark wood.

10

The color of *you shall go no further*. Where, in the underbelly of the Wolf—for all cities are wolves—even rust is contested terrain.

11

Intermission. The way closed eyes recompose light.

12

I am waiting with my staff at the edge of the Poem. I have followed a cloud called God. Behind me, the armies of a king I could not slay.

13

The king I loved.

SIXTEEN

Dre's Chronic is the only time
            he leans   head back
        the humming plank   unearths
                    tender brown neck
bruised
            you watch   smoke's sorcery
        weave a bullet's song
    from the nest of his lungs   almost hear
a horizon's whine silvered by Soviet
        fighter-bombers   taste
venom of unborn
                    love   the black hole
        war carves in a body

                            he will speak once
before language   Kabul
            running to where his father &
    other mujahedeen were lowered
        scorched ground in prayer mats
                    no instruction manual
                        no dialectic to mouthfuls
    of dust   you masticate
                collateral damage   meaning
        domesticate   ask to mend
                    bones still breaking
        inside you   pilgrim
                of chrome & knuckled glance
                    make your imprint
            a shard of fire   if

one golden summer
                you agree to believe
        love can hold explosives
            love is as strong as the land
                        love is this jaw of a boy
        who pins you facedown
            by the nape   and through
whose fist you will enter
        your haunting meaning *somebody*
                better get this bitch

                        can you wrest the day's
            moon from a cloud of moths
                        thicket of Nike'd ankles
baseball-capped heads turned
                    the other way   can you never
                            ask yourself
            what you would have done
the sky & the fire forever equal
                    parts of your heart   if
        the poem will come
            the choice
                    to give away
        what you will not learn
                        to live without

the first winter is gunmetal that slips
in and out of the bones

the first winter hurts like arroyos
in the sour, sunless brain

the first winter flakes the elbows
like tobacco

the first winter dries the phlegm
on the back of the tongue

the first winter teaches girls
to feed themselves to the wolves

the first winter is Ganesh
ramming his tusks at the radio

the first winter is a fiction of green
threads knotted into mercy

the first winter thinks of meth & diapers
arms in the damp wood

the first winter is a stopped clock
my father's wheelchair

rolling to the edge of the roof

WINTER COUNTRY

Red-knuckled, my city stands
my wind emptied of flags.

Weeds, like disbelief,
sprout through car windows
by the train tracks.

O, ice
bestial heart
holding back the panic & confetti

though sometimes I light small fires
watch smoke tunnel through
the broken roofs like angels

you are the lone survivor
    mirrors in the train's path
      the only ceasefire
      I know.

PROMISED LAND: SONNETS FOR MY MOTHER

I

Wake to the violin of leaves. Before light's vein
ruptures night's harem of sirens and red-eye crows,
pull dark deep in your lungs, wash your face in shadows.
A thick cloth between you and the wolves in your brain
rends inch by whitening inch. Breath's hunger for rain
nooses the sallow air, seams the hush of pillows
made silken by sweat, your body's heat the bruised rose
giving up its fleshy *please* to a prayer's cane.
In real time, the strings you hear are water,
your mother's hand the bow gliding it to crescendo.
Arched over steel she scours what cannot be sung back
to their unscarred state: plates, bowls, the chipped decanter
your father bought at a garage sale years ago
when his calling was certain as ink's garb of black.

II

How to hear God's call among the black thousand
hungers that needle flesh into a single cry,
sleet of bodiless wings, a riven tongue of sky?
Flight is the armored wind prowling his shadow, sand
spilling out of its eye sockets. He feels its hand
in the wrench of dung-crusted dokar wheels, the sigh
of kites ruffling crowns of coconut trees, the lie
of a homeland as the heart's rest. How do they stand
up, twenty pews away from each other without
ever trading a single glance, when a man they
have never seen before asks, *who believes here*
with all of the words they have never braved aloud,
all the names and lengths of skin they have gnawed away,
in land where milk and honey can sweeten fear?

III

Like milk and honey, fear clotted the moon's rays
when credit ran lean as canned soup, staying warm meant
sitting in church four nights a week and paying rent
shackled her to a decade of twelve-hour days,
six-day weeks at the sweatshop two hours away.
Winter, stuttered benediction of knuckles, lent
snow's chaos of pronouns to her already bent
tongue, loaves of discount bread frozen for months and gray
she swallowed without chewing. Faith, raised to duty,
is made for such times as these when you must grope blind
for shoes in the cement of night, trick aching bones
to lurch with the bus, listen to your mouth empty
of meaning every time you try to cross the line
between you and daughters goldening into stones.

IV

Between gold and the stone's grammar: hand and table,
roof and mirror, shoe rack, staples and tins of Spam,
signatures, carpet, margarine and bitter jam,
fumes and frayed gloves, how fog rinses pine and cable,
the cardboard, scissors, leather a man is able
to incarnate at will by nuance of a door slam,
and girls like dandelions who bleed and bedlam
the light-polluted skies with the speed of Babel.
Between slat and rain, between tongues, we designed,
my sister and I, brick of cloth, voice of fur,
our own pop culture of microwaveable silt
and decapitated Barbies. We swam and mined
drawls for our midnight radio, cranked it to blur
their marathons of blame: our near-plastic guilt.

V

Don't talk to me about guilt. Or the way shame sounds
like a plastic-coated man shuffling behind you,
toothless and with stones in his fists. Orpheus who
is not quite dead, sitting up in his pool of brown
guts to pluck a harp. You make choices around
those pus-yellow eyes. When I say protection, you
want a naked sort of body. When I say true,
I mean a weeping willow. What's under a gown
of ice. I mean there's never been a time to speak
out of turn. Surely not at sunset, when a man
you've pleaded for all your life is wrestling to part
with his. Test the weight leaking out of his skin. Streak
his glass walls with your fingerprints. You will, you can
call him father. Look, look at the bruise in his heart.

VI

After, we learn that the bruise is a rogue singing
heart, its idiom blue in green, a single lace
of light on wingtips and freshly tossed dirt, like grace
released under breath to a deserted room. Bring
lavender. A watch. His second best tie. The ring
vowing you to a mountain's silence and the trace
of a grandchild he would never warm with his gaze
like his still lives back on the island, still hanging
on the peeled walls. What does a sun ray sound like
through the vaults of skin, bouncing off the varnished cold,
rifling through the rain's silver earrings and alcoves
of feather? What does it promise to breach the dike
of fierce, maternal clouds; what does it withhold?
Your refusals become her eyes' trembling wolves.

VII

You tremble in the wolfish dim, drunk on the blood
beading your spine's rim. Your palms are cradling your brow,
your palms are smoke. The Antillean is half prow,
half fin, humming ribbons of white sand, rolling bud
in one hand while the other gauges how to stud
the animal's sheathed claw in your vertebrae, how
to defy borders of muscle and vein to plow
the proud flesh with amber, indigo, onyx. Mud
shifts inside you, like false memory: did not both
Kafka's condemned man and his punisher commit
themselves to the harrow? Did they not aim to strike
against disappearance? Like a gesture, the oath
washing into air, you conjure again the pit
of her burnt song inside you, the calling's last spike.

VIII

A burnt song. A dawn's silvery spike. A murmur
like leaves or fingers in water. A lung of strings.
A warning's siren. A prayer that leaves nothing
to fortune. A plate of warm bread. A stray daughter
asleep and returned to the hearth. A scarred river
of lights overflowing its banks with each passing
minute. A mirror and arrows of ash darting
through her hair. A thirst to follow, now a whisper
on her Bible's threadbare pages. You hear her turn
the tap off, slip on the sturdy work shoes and search
for the keys. This will be the seventeenth year she's
yielded ruins inside her to love's brazen urn
before another day on the belt. This small church
where to rise is to bear the ground under your knees.

SELF-PORTRAIT AS THE LAST WILL OF LOT'S WIFE

Should angels come and break
bread at your table, garbed in the frailty
of men, do not ask how you might ransom

a city which never stops burning
even as its ashes harden into the candled arch
of your mouth. Once I harbored

wood and silver in my blood, walked
long nights alone in fields of hyssop dragging
the moon like a rag behind me.

Once I pressed darkness to my eyes
like a salve against the smooth pulsing bodies:
my daughters poured out like wine

at the blessed gates. I heard Lot's voice,
Do what you like with them, but not to these men
under my roof's protection.

A woman's flesh has never been less
than a purgatory of salt, the treacherous plain
you haste through without looking back.

So let it be painted as vanity this body I face
toward the fury of angels; let memory make of me
a scream that wasn't there.

REMISSION

Between Gospel and the belt, a daughter learns her lines.
Each mote in her father's eye she reads to learn her lines.

A pure faith: impossible without hypocrisy!
Even more for immigrants, who have not learned their lines.

He'd sing each hymn as though it were ransom for his life.
The child he'd hold too long, refusing to learn her lines.

I fell into a paddy field. The leeches grew fat
on my belly and thighs. Bloodlust quickly learned my lines.

Bent double from stiff winters and the debt of nations
poems too get heavy; hang low as they learn their lines.

How much exile is enough? How many treeless
plains before the hands wither trying to learn their lines?

When his body began to die, he said, "The fruit of
prayer is fire." Ashes—see if you can learn their lines.

The homeless share much in common with birds. Feast of crumbs;
flight. Voices that unclothe language won't learn its lines.

Then I saw light kiss the smooth skull, cobalt country of
veins: a door left ajar, when he was learning his lines.

How could I choose your epitaph? I'm no Samuel,
who heeded Jehovah in the stone and learned his lines.

A man who becomes his own memory, like the belt
will not sting again nor learn another body's lines.

Look how empty this moonlight is. *Come unto me and
I will give you rest.* Pa, your daughter has learned her lines.

PULSES

begin the body's wick
    the kidney-root of flame

    muscular palimpsest   my father's
      lips a memory of water

    hold vigil around the bed
         become garden
      float and bless
            life's effort to lift

      the dark helmet:

(a) he throbbed like a mountain range
(b) cold is a field of tulips somewhere in northern Washington

    the sky empties of conviction
        each downward stroke
           a bony green   frost
      simultaneous char

        there are waves we cannot
   resist   waves like God's

   fingernails dragged
      across a veil:

(c) field of insects, sheen of eyes, field of frozen lightning
(d) O, petal, please defend the yellow, the red, the purple, the blue

see the son he was
    the lineage of winds that made
        refugee of his heart

hands folded now   immune
        to shadows in the corners
  of his mind only velvet

                tulips
    thicken calcify   knuckles
split at the seams   walls
    of the damage taken

        apart:

(e) a smile is a perfectly tied shoelace, a black windbreaker
(f) with blue fleece collar the body pushes out

his salt in the bowl of my neck
        newly formed
   plateau on earth   from one
     absence
           to another

what is weight   what is human
    but the blinking of tulips

      around a small downed moon?

(g) both the skin of the egg and the hair caught in a bun are efforts
(h) to bind memory

father   my head, we are
    twin fruits gnarled into one
      the neck our pulses
          beat in battle

mother   a mesh of nights is thrown
                over your cheeks a country
            which will not leave
                    my body:

(i) we are always approaching the edge of a foreign land
(j) we are no less afraid

        of the sweetness left
                    for bees to redeem
        stamen knuckles the dust
                gathering force   our love

                this wind-bowed grass

PORTRAIT OF MY FATHER AS A PIANIST

Behind disinfected curtains,
     beyond touch of sunrise
devouring the terrible gold

     of leaves, a man could be
his own eternal night. City
     flattened to rubble, his

surviving height a black flight
     of notes: the chip-toothed
blade and oldest anesthetic.

     Escaped convict, he climbs
wild-eyed, one hand out—
     running its twin on the rails

of a broken Steinway. Who
     has not been found guilty
of a carrion cry—the dream

     of a feathered departure
one has not earned, then fall
     back down teeming fault lines

of the flesh? Memory recedes
     into nocturne, a kingdom born
of spruce and fading light—

     he reaches in the end what
he had to begin with: fingertips
     on corrupted tissue, cathedral

of octaves in his thinning
        breath, tears like small stubborn
gods refusing to fall.

POEM FOR PRISONER #46664

In dimness before the night shift, half-dressed
on a spit-stained bed, I cut my finger on the page describing
the milk you left to sour on the window ledge;

a small obeisance to the human part that wants, needs
to say, "I prefer this, not that," as you stroll silently through
someone else's furniture, planting bombs in apartheid

then risking all of it for a taste of the man who is still sweat,
hurt, a galaxy of longing—the man and not the lion.
The baby sucks my breast dry and in the void,

dogs bark. I think of the choices fathers and husbands make
in places where their families live hunted, hungry,
rabid with fear; where the rich and government are

synonymous with natural disasters—*nothing you can do
about it but buckle down and mourn the dead*—I think
of the ways men disappear, into wages, drink, sometimes if

they fight, into symbols. Then our memories of them must be
less important than their sacrifice. I think about the choices
mothers and wives have, to birth and to bury, to be left

behind, piecing lives out of split threads and absences,
to follow, to burn. Every time I stand in my bones and feel
lost, a stranger; every time I shield my face in the dark

I know it is because my ancestors chose to run. To leave
no trace on the windowsills we passed through. Madiba,
if it were not for you, this cut reddening the words

in the dumb light, I might have never learned to say, *Fear,*
I am not a lamb on your altar. This here I touch
with my body, make holy with language

all the arms of wreckage, this we who will not be moved.

HOWL IN OUR HANDS

And that huge rose of ours   our only bewilderment
our offense   on earth our balcony
                                              on the kingdom of heaven

—Fady Joudah, "Tell Life"

ARBORETUM

Two women beneath a weeping
cherry in full bloom. One brushes

earth with her hair, deciphering
the calligraphy of fallen petals.

The other lifts her face to sun, laced
by branch and flowers like tiny

palms of snow. Almost a postcard
of spring, who could guess

the bounty on their heads, the men
with knives behind, how they listen

for their lives in what will never
be said. Give thanks. If only today

the world is their sons rolling
down hills of grass, the boughs

bending around them like mercy.

AFTER COLTRANE

The boy, in the brandy light of a passing train, unlatches
a black case, the surface of which is regret, hauls out
the curled studded bronze parts and assembles what
desire is plotting to make his tongue's chariot.

When spit has saturated the reed, his mother
sits beside him, a hinge; her hands tiny iron gates that swing
open then shut to the galloping chords, as though guarding
an island of ghosts. Near its shore floats her at his age,

water lapping chin, chlorine rusting windpipe.
She has always trusted herself to be a boat, empowered
to part her own reflection, still she finds the body engulfed—
arms blown glass, air like planets breaking the orbit of her mouth.

No one's taught her to drown with grace, or grip the breath
which like a python squeezes the jelly-life of the lungs, before lunging,
pure freedom, toward the surface, the rudder-blades of sun
that slash and slash yet never scar the darkness, that god

of failed rebellions. She rubs the memory, a coin of bone
between her breasts. Who knows how long she was there,
kissed by linoleum, in the heart of distortion, not thinking to plead
for her life? The way her son holds his breath, secretly

chains to a single note all the mutinies inside him—
she wants nothing more than to say, *Here, here I am*
to this sound at once roof and typhoon, heaven and the race
of wildfire to which all flesh at last gives, in tribute, in blues.

SIEGE: IN RESPONSE TO THE MAN WHO ASKED ME, "WHERE IS THE COURAGE IN YOUR POETRY?"

I

Courage considers this planet of paper and gravity from a dust-knit corner.

Courage does not open the mail, or pay the rent.

Between the ebb and swell of iron, courage writes poems about war and capitalism and trees.

II

War and *capitalism* and *trees* are as much adhesives as metaphors, courage learns. They enter the world gowned, trusted, unlike *rape*, *after-rape*, or *fire-resistant bodies*.

Courage knows language is the alchemy Isaac Newton sought and could not solve. If truly courageous, it might go further to claim language is the only hubris.

Thus *desire* takes on the names of cities, and *stone* the songs of the vanquished. Thus *war* becomes human and *rape* becomes woman.

Courage is full of angry rap, and collects words like "fugue" and "sylph" to organize fissures around the details of being twenty-four years old, bloodstained dick in hand, mirror choking with steam, and water gunning down the way a woman sounds behind a wall.

III

Around the neon fiefdom of a Motel 6, the night was lanced by stars and irreversible decisions.

In the way he showed up late to teach her a lesson.
In the way she beat his chest *stop* and shut her knees like a bear trap.

If courage acquired a genealogy, it would include the four-hour drive he made every Friday from Fort Lewis across the US–Canada border to where she lived with the kid that wasn't his. The winter he slept in a truck outside her house; their hasty, cramped fucking behind curtains of snow.

He was immortal then.
An opened envelope of flesh.

IV

Courage is a forensics analyst.
The night is a Led Zeppelin howl.
Decisions are our only witnesses.

Commit to a cleansing of the self, to auditing the ledgers of the soul.

Which at certain times of the day, while idling in traffic, or watching a porn flick on mute, clouds up like dozens of men who have not bathed in months, tedium, their scalps crawling with tiny fires beneath combat helmets, sand in the gaps of their teeth crusting their balls, their nerves guitar strings stretched across oceans of forgetting.

He said they were taught to make themselves come before pulling the trigger.

V

Memory is looking back. This is not memory.

On the threadbare cover, in Jezebel lips, eyes like bullet rims, breasts defiant and engraved by his fingers. "Like a pianist's," she told him years ago, kissing their tips, believing them capable of music beneath their habit for destruction.

Courage looks up at the moon like a bright neck, and thinks of what it would be like to fold this paper planet into a blade,   and swing.

VI

The way shadow betrays the presence of light, there is a murderer behind this one, and one behind that one, and so on, death confronting death, back and back and back, to the time giants were made defenseless, Odysseus a cripple in the rocks. Back to the apple's origin, toppled cathedral of God's mind, the inconsolable cell of the universe.

In the room: suitcase with international tags. Nikes and flowered skirt. Wallets, mints, library cards.

In the room: the salt-whipped animal of sight, panting, fighting for its life.

VII

For years courage writes about everything but this, learning twenty-two different ways to say "orange."

Isn't courage at least an orphan of repetition? Persistence? (Stupidity?)
When he returned like a wet god, she was still there. They lay beside each other through the night and listened to headboards moan against the barracks of sleep. The next day they cashed in coupons for the water park resort, ate sushi, and listened to Chris Rock on Pandora,

and laughed.

A kingdom bloomed in her.
It was made of string and mica, vinegar,
the clean-picked ribs of love. She grew into a forest,

she could not be found.

VIII

If he didn't love his mother, and father, and brother, and sister, and nieces, and
nephews,
if he didn't love his country, he might confess everything.

Instead, he broke what he could. And if he could, he would wrinkle that which
he has broken into a song. The song would become a classic. A homeless demon
prowling the television waves, the teeth of boys

itching to be men.

IX

Does asking for forgiveness make a poem courageous?
Can the poem like a spool of thread thrown into the night deliver
the punished and punishing self?

Is the poem ascension?
A stake through memory? A mask? A search party?

What is left but the poem, if he is already a song, and she will never be
whole, or believed, or safe, or reflected—what good, what remedy

is courage?

X

It is raining today: the sky, the bodies on the grass, the process of revision, all mirror the river's stones.

Courage has not stepped out of the house for months.
Courage rations each cup of coffee and sips the last muddy dredges on earth.

On smoke and dark grains, laboring with a single word.

On smoke and dark grains, a series of small, carefully timed erosions.
A voice behaving like a wound.
An I.

AUBADE

When the wedding was over, the witnesses gone,
the wine-stained dress back in the arms of its maker,

we drove down to Monterey, forty-degree weather
to test the eternity we had sworn to. I thought I heard

the ghosts of Mack and Eddie laughing in the trees
as we fumbled for warmth, suddenly cruel, clumsy

with each other in the middle of a room dazed by
its own genealogy: mahogany armoire and wrought

iron table, Victorian sofa in navy-rose print, cupids
engraved in the oak bed—cheeks flaring hallelujah

at redcoats on the wall whose rifles are trained on
coppery men with wrists tied behind their backs—,

a gold-leaf frame. Moths flickered: scraps of news
from another world ablaze on the spinal cord of night

as though they too had touched the fury of our fathers,
when we as children crushed earlobes into fists

as they dug pits in our mothers, who endured and kept
enduring, who mended themselves like old uniforms

that would not be outgrown. We came as though
nakedness wasn't at once a forked road and the fury

drawing its noose around us. I want to believe the sun
hovered in the lark's throat before it flew away,

before we saw the white wall rise behind each other's
eyes, remnant from when we held a howl in our hands

and tried to write the story of forgiveness.

RES DOMESTICA

You swear I erode you.
My love, there are doors that weep.
Children who survive on wild gardenia.
Men who do not recover   after they've seen
        the lightning hidden in their sleeves.

I want to tell you the truth.   No other has stood
behind these gates, though tempests come and go

        like fathers.   Mornings too were here

with birdsong and berries, though I never asked where
they went when their colors ceased
                                to warm the wood.

Look out the window.   The city is a sea
of bread knives and designer boots,

                                        pilgrims who've lost
their literacy of the stars. When this metaphor ends,
what is left of us to worship?

I am not a wise woman. I give thanks for the simplest things:

a swift cut through the many bodies of the onion,
the best-before date, which does not mean expiration,
how the shock of cotton fresh out of the dryer reminds me

        I am charged with a power I cannot see.

And maybe it's Tupac or the constant drizzle
that makes me believe I owe iron
to the men   walking their bones so cautiously
around puddles, dogs, one another.

But I look at your hands studded by bits of garlic.
There has always been the life

we unpeel. Embalm in the juice of olives.

I have not been left
stripped in a metal bowl.   This is the closest I've come
                                        to fire.

I still don't know the best place
to eat.

THE ARGUMENT

Call it paranoia or narcissism, but I swear the moon is
eyeballing me through the window's grime. I said, "No,
the bed is not a random search," and all the tiny hairs
on my arms stand up in protest. On the grand stage
of the train station across the street, a man is playing
out a scene from *Hamlet*, a bottle in place of the ghost
of his father. The single source of light in this room,
a reading lamp bought at Target after we flew our lives
across the forty-ninth parallel, is an egg-colored fist bravely
pumping its yolk into the charcoal silence between us.
Look, by now the rice has dried, each grain stuck fast
to the dinner plates, which will be hell to wash later,
and I can't stop thinking about that motherfucker
Kliney, who masterminded the great escape of 1945
from Eastern State Penitentiary. Skinny, nondescript,
with posture like a bent wire, when he spoke syllables
rattled like dice in his cheeks. The guards trusted him
with maintenance duty and he dug a twelve-foot-deep,
hundred-foot-long tunnel from cell block seven to just
outside the fifteen-foot-thick prison wall, electric lights
and all. The labor alone took eighteen months and he was
recaptured in three hours. Which is about how long we've
been at it this time, bracketed only by the pathetic
chirping of our son's Nintendo DS. I am so afraid of
being seen. At Knight Park, there are trees that will not
make it through the winter, but no HELP WANTED sign
on the Christmas-lit store windows. This morning I saw
a fire-breasted bird in the backyard. It could have been
a metonym for the frost. I'm still betting on it to sing.

TIME STOPS ON MOUNT BATUR

In one version of the story, she never made it to the peak.
There was the ice of a thousand darts.
Red light dying against the moss.
A ceramic glass of tea: steaming, jasmine.

> *Some of the tourists—beefy, pink-nosed, zipped up to their chins—*
> *watched her pee behind the crumbling rampart where barefoot women,*
> *babies suckling at their breasts, sold corn nuts and bottled Coca-Cola.*

"How shall I describe the stars to you? It's as if God had been
punched in the face and his teeth sprayed across the sky."

On the rotting wood one cigarette after another
she was a thin blanket
wrapped around juts of bone.

> *There was the blue water below, sober, spoonlike*
> *the way she imagined each particle of lung. The mist dense as dust*
> *that lay at night between her and the husband.*

There was after all the old man who extended his hand
like a freshly sanded tabletop, and pulled her up
over the blade-sharp edge. Her grip was solid,
her feet bled, she could have made the scramble

on her own. "I took it to be kind
so he wouldn't think I thought myself too good
but of course he expected to get paid."

The brambles had fingernails like her mother's.
They waltzed on her face and arms like soldiers at their last
ball before the war. Her neck felt like
a subway tunnel echoing with rats.

Banana sandwiches.
Raw eggs that broke and made her palms stick
in reluctant prayer.
The ice of a thousand darts piercing
the body's ember.

Enter the green-walled kitchen with the broken light bulb.
The saturation of garlic in the walls like a secret
ancestry. There are the finely shaped legs, irascible hair,
the barely perceptible film of grease on the clean pots and pans.

In another version, she listened to the guide's warning and, torn
feet and all, threw her bones into the tar-darkness like flares.
Of course she was thinking of the book, the son, the coming winter.
Of course things drown at great heights.

"Where are you? Where did you go? Why have you come back?"
He is earnest as a seagull scanning the waves.
The silence hangs between them, a curtain of bees.

There was no way to cheat how steep it was.
Or the blackness of the ash, which had crystallized to sand
pouring warmly, needling the lines of the palms.
"The angle of the climb was such that I couldn't look all the way

down." Who was she trying to fool?
Dawn was delayed for over an hour. No electricity.
She heard voices like swinging lanterns and couldn't see

a damn thing. Her fingers refuse to uncurl.
It seems silly to say, "Well, the sun was a juvenile act of arson,
it was quickly put out in the fog," or
"I could have used a ladder."

Other versions are possible, maybe.
She's not sure which to tell.
In another one the pretty guide gives everyone the finger,
quits, and goes home to her daughter and her man,
who teaches by day and is a sharecropper by 3:00 P.M.

They never speak of the woman who left her skin all over the mountainside.

TABUH RAH

I

After the wounds are scraped
the blood flaked to sawdust
the feathers black snow
around her ankles, she will

bite into the bird and drink
like a coyote or child of Cain,
roll the sour heat
across her tongue; she will

become a weapon.

II

The loose bolt of the jugular.
The wrench of the tongue.
Inside her the hands of men

churn like Pacific storms.
Gleam of coin toss, then the rat-tat-tat
polemics of a dead revolution.

III

The bets are placed.
Tourists fiddle with their cameras.
The cocks are thrown into the pit,

armed with their bodies,
slick with god:

whatever knife plays within us,
what Lorca called *duende*,
will mark its territory tonight.

IV

The spectacle cleanses the witness.
Tradition and formlessness both

demand a good death. When it is over,
the sun like a fat white spider

resumes its weaving, in and out
of Bintang beer bottles, the ditches

where children bathe, the wax paper
kites that pin up the sky.

V

She sucks the bones dry.
Each flightless bird's eye that will not close again.
In the caves of memory,
where light is also memory,
one finds one's way
fingering the cold walls,
the charred feathers of the dead.
She will press herself against them, unyielding:

To love depends on this.

FROM A TALISMAN'S POINT OF VIEW

All the world is kindling, a brain ticking towards
the consummate light, black light man will claim as his
beginning. Stars tenuous as chalk on a cave wall,

destruction so loud it can only spore into timeless
horns of silence. The swamps gasp open:
egg, gristle, indigo-beating heart, the hairy carapace

in halls of fire ice grass. I drip down the bark,
gather them like notes in the slow syrup of grief. Become
the skin of a song no memory will survive, seraphim

of twigs, knots in rock and seabed, blood of furnaces,
incense. In spring the waves throw up my life
into the baskets of midwives and fishermen. I will inspire

warships. The drops of sun on a bride's ears, around
her neck and ankles. I will blaze with her through
the duty-bound nights. Of conifer, agathis, hymenaea,

the blue-gummed earth where minor thieves of light
are chewed into a flawed, shining inheritance:
gravediggers, god makers, both will call me tears.

BREACH

While other girls were testing
the firm peach of their bodies against
Apollo's golden shield, I was looking for ways
to tear out of mine like a wet suit.
To swim away, bold and magenta fish
far beyond the Pharaoh's hook of my father's pain, the hollow
floor of the boat where he waited like a great immovable
kedge in the gull's cry and bright green foam
of my childhood. I believed in him, believed
in the fate of fish, to sift the planet's most plentiful
element through their bodies and be reeled in by hunger,
to smash against wood, metal, and be buried in ice
for distant mouths to swill in fiery wine, to enter
the void with open eyes. I walked
in my body—like a long tan belt dragged it
through the teeth and laws of men, the hotel rooms
of their hearts, cocks like the staff of Moses which gulped down
the kingly cobras, to see what would
flake away or continue their dim existences
beneath the migrant furniture, the power of the poison
of my own making. And I am not Christ or the Buddha
but I know what it is try to climb out
of the body, its walls of moss and melanin
by deprivation or desecration the wish
to quit standing in the middle of it like Jupiter's hurricane
raging without end, the red navel, the hurt
that is topography and blueprint, crew and ship.
I have pushed and pushed this body against the lips of fire,
observed bruises bloom like a reluctant spring,
and after my son was born I sank into it like quicksand
on the blue sky of the hospital bed, the raft of frozen bandages,

blood that poured over the flogged hills like a royal army,
blood that besieged. For months
I thought about sitting still, about gravity doing its work
as nerve ends bared themselves across the abyss life had burst
through, months glistening in the clit's moon and tides
of the labia like needles. When you kiss me
there, like a man who loves his woman in spite of her
galaxy of scars, when you tongue the remains
of the pyre into a banquet fit for warriors about to embark
on the longest journey of their lives, you are saying
what language never will, that I am
safe, worthy—that I never should have been
broken into by force.

TONIGHT WE DRINK WHISKEY & DIVE

Over the balcony rail, two hundred feet up,
I watch my brothers walk to the liquor store.
It's spring—the sun has just poured its last
russet malt over the ice of the Rockies,
and the air is laced with reggae, cop sirens,
kids shouting across islands of concrete.
We've been discussing what it means to be

poets of color, how we often feel obligated
to make the agonies of our communities dance
(to paraphrase Baraka), to take sides in wars
we had hoped our poetry would help us
transcend. And how still, our bodies divide,
though we burst at the seams, into costumes
of power and desire we spend our lives

repairing: we men, we women. Now the dark
lifts its woolen head, a sapphire god. My poet-
brothers almost imperceptibly hunch their
shoulders, dig hands into pockets, shifting
their route to blend into the densest shadows.
I see Hari's cigarette go out, Seve's Kangol
a drifting temple. Then for a split second, a net

of crows swoops low over them, and I flinch.
How can I say I love these men, when I've only
touched them through the skin of conquest?
Beyond their swagger, which grows smaller
and smaller as they cross further into the night,
I see the mountain peaks. Regal and jagged,
in their shade I've begged, fought, knelt, and

won my voice, though I've not praised the faces
they lift so reverently to dynamite, the tracks
laid across them like scars. Soon the men will
return, laughter and shit-talk rippling against
the glass, the brown liquid of them spilling
from lips and over the rail. We'll slip back
into the play, the third act, as though poetry

made us invincible to the ending, as though
poetry could save us from falling.

SALVAGE

May heart, hewn and ocean-deep,
     harvest your parts
thrown by blast, rock of empire-hum.

May eardrum, ribboned, unfurling
     stir to the colors
of need, the purples of soil and stone.

May neck, vapor, petaled as the rose
     shadow each kiss
blown into wind, against distance.

May knee, vector, rude evidence
     of longing, hollow
in history bowls of dirt and holy water.

May wrist, soul's fallen minaret,
     litany of fated
spins, release the ghosts of dance.

May eye, temple of desire, feast
     on the root of light
un-absolved, vein of sun, fugitive.

May skin, animal, insignia of fire
     ground to dust
find passage in the breath of leaves.

May bone, sacred text within
     of ache, un-sayings
spell at last, rest. At last, belonging.

May memory, navel of the lost
       arm of the vanished,
rise. Wide-eyed, mortal, a whole world

moving against redemption.

EPILOGUE

Only, the instant you lay hold of earth,
discard it, cast it far, far out from shore
and turn away.
> —Homer, *Odyssey*

(*mirrors*)

In early hours the house

is reflection, a hint of light
        where the body charts
     around history's ravening
       crowds and chimeras

a path to itself. I wake
      to the wonder
    we have not all perished
       keeping up appearances

for the blind moon's sake.
        There are flashes of bird
    behind the glass. A sun

in the solid mist. Must not there be
       reasons if we mine
    deep enough the rockblood

we were given?

(*vertigoes*)

The truth is I saw myself

        in her oily coveralls, missing fingernails
    hair like ink spilled against the wall

when I handed her the soap & towel
pretending not to see
     the syringe on the floor,
the half-used cylinder of blush
she clutched like a relic.

        you can't send me in there
          they are watching

I know the story. Hear
     the cameras clicking in my skull, rain
forming fragile, self-enclosed worlds on the Plexiglas
each its own obituary of light
                The truth is

I saw the cost of freedom

      I know you're watching

    her fury so thick & red I could
      smear it with my thumb

(*diversions*)

For seconds I am caught in the capsule of its scream
     the train rushing in the opposite direction, its windows
          the gills of a burning harmonica, toward the fluorescence

and uniformed men, insinuations of order and preferable
     sonorant of regret, the day which begins and ends in the same
          landscape of desire: scuffed shoes, plastic bags, lolled heads.

I run. Away from the station into caverns behind the face
     I hide from passersby, into the slap of heels against concrete
          then packed dirt—my heart dappled by leaves pregnant with

sap, dangling with the famine of insects. I push sinews
     like cracked urns through the opaque steam of the lungs,
          lacquered veins, the swarm of splintered, open nerves

where my son tore out his first cry before I was eighteen.
     Away, away into myself, where each insinuation of light
          glints like a carbine and the stench of ammonia clings to

memory's black roots. What but the poem can teach me
     to scavenge like geese with their casually folded wings
          knowing exactly what they are and where they should

lower their tongues to the earth? Or be my joy like the eastern
     phoebe bathing in a muddy pool, sharing her reflection with
          the worm and the lice, surrendering all to the terrors of the light?

(*insurgencies*)

The road circles back to the house

    where I read that the poet Lynda Hull died at forty

    She'd have nothing but contempt for you, guilty and standing here
    long past the last train, waiting for the police sweep,
    waiting for the clamp on the wrist

    Still, I feel a kinship because we both committed

        a kind of treason
        (against slender destiny / we rowed

    far beyond the last candle, the evacuated
    pages as though our hands were

        thunder / mere eddies
    of audible lives) Which might lead

to poetry: the kind of beauty that incinerates
        the shelter of the body, *the form of this hunger*

within   To feed on ruin, milk-dark nights, the bones

    of beginnings.

The italicized lines in the section "(*insurgencies*)" are from Lynda Hull's poems "Gateway to Manhattan" and "Studies from Life," respectively, both from her *Star Ledger*.

Acknowledgments

With thanks to the editors of the following publications where these poems first appeared, some in their earlier versions:

Apogee Journal: "Suppose You Were a Komodo Dragon" "Tabuh Rah," "Though We've No Chance of Escape, Encore"

As Us: "Garden State," "The Men Who Turned Into Air," "Time Stops on Mount Batur"

bedfellows: "Aubade," "Sixteen"

Big Bell: "Elegy for the Hellfire," "Lazarus Reconsiders His Awakening"

Black Renaissance/Renaissance Noire: "Promised Land: Sonnets for My Mother"

The Collapsar: "The Argument"

Dismantle: An Anthology of Writing from the VONA/Voices Writing Workshop: "Poem for Prisoner #46664"

Dusie: "For Khalil, First Responder, Whose Name Means 'Friend'"

Fifth Wednesday Journal: "How to Watch *The Act of Killing*," "Self-Portrait as the Last Will of Lot's Wife"

jmww: "Jesus Is Tested in the Downtown Eastside" (as "God Lives in the Downtown Eastside")

Kalyani Magazine: "Salvage" (as "Balm for the Un-Body"), "Siege: In Response to the Man Who Asked Me, 'Where Is the Courage in Your Poetry?' "

Kweli Journal: "After Hurricane Sandy"

The Massachusetts Review: "The American Dream Writes to Orpheus"

Obsidian: "After Coltrane," "Tonight We Drink Whiskey & Dive"

Ozone Park Journal: "Res Domestica"

Painted Bride Quarterly: "Breach," "From a Talisman's Point of View," "Pulses," "Winter Country"

Read Women: An Anthology: "Anthem," "Ishtar in Suburbia"

Terrain.org: "Arboretum," "Merapi"

The Wide Shore: "Elegy for Red: A *Zuihitsu*"

~

We speak, they say, of a new country, a new love
that no one had conceived.
—RAÚL ZURITA, "THE SNOW"

I am grateful for the gathering of voices—present and past—that helped make this book possible.

Thanks to the writers whom I have not known in person but whose light guided my way—Pramoedya Ananta Toer, Chairil Anwar, Frantz Fanon, Theresa Hak Kyung Cha, Audre Lorde, Adrienne Rich, Raúl Zurita, Rainer Maria Rilke, Amiri Baraka, Derek Walcott, Mahmoud Darwish, Paul Celan, Gwendolyn Brooks, Lucille Clifton, Denise Levertov, Larry Levis, Galway Kinnell, Marina Tsvetaeva, and Lynda Hull, among many others.

Special thanks to Joy Harjo, Willie Perdomo, Aracelis Girmay, Patrick Rosal, Jimmy Santiago Baca, Jeffery Renard Allen, and Eleanor Wilner—whose wisdom, friendship, and mentorship helped me grow alongside these poems.

To Voices of Our Nations (VONA) and the Vermont Studio Center, thank you for giving me space, time, and sacred communities to write in. To Vern Miller—so proud to be part of the Fifth Wednesday team. Thank you for believing in me! I am also immensely grateful to Asian Arts Initiative and the Leeway Foundation for supporting my vision and development as an artist.

To my writing family—Hari Alluri, Seema Reza, Nico Amador, and Marissa Johnson-Valenzuela—and my comrades at New Sanctuary Movement and Grassroots Global Justice—thank you for holding me accountable not only to the best version of myself, but also to the courage, clarity and love our collective liberation demands.

To Parneshia Jones, for delivering this book to the world, for expanding and challenging our republic of poetry with such fierceness and vision; Ellen Hagan, for reading this manuscript with unfathomable generosity; and the rest of the publishing team at Northwestern University Press—I cannot thank you all enough.

To my family—you are the reason. You have always been the reason. I write to rejoin you, to be with you across the distances over which we have been scattered; to be the daughter, sister, and kin that you deserve.

To Seve—if I have the capacity today to live fearlessly and in hope, it is because I am facing that life with you. And Paul—how can I thank you for sharing your mother with poetry? Every day, the love I could not have conceived begins anew, with you.